# Games Galore
## for
# Baby Showers

*80+ fun games and activities*
*(brand new ideas and traditional favorites)*
*to celebrate baby's arrival*

## by Shari Ann Pence

## Illustrated by: Shelley Dieterichs

**Funcastle®**
**publications**

*Riverside, California*

First Edition

Library of Congress Control Number: 2006932912

ISBN 13 978-0-9645771-4-5
ISBN 10 0-9645771-4-3

Funcastle Publications
P.O. Box 51217
Riverside, CA 92517
(951) 653-5200
**www.partygamesgalore.com**

Manufactured in the United States of America

Notice: Although the games and activities contained in this book have been tested and researched to the best of our ability, individual results may vary. All recommendations and suggestions are made without any guarantees on the part of the author or Funcastle Publications. The author and publisher disclaim all liability incurred in connection with the use of this information.

*Dedicated to all moms*
*and mom's-to-be*
*who wish to shower*
*their baby with*
*a joyous celebration*

*A very special thank you*
*to my daughter,*
*Sarah,*
*for content editing, contributions,*
*layout design assistance and technical support.*
*You are a very bright and gifted mom-to-be!*

# Table of Contents

# *Introduction*

Celebrating the arrival of a new baby is a time for family and friends to share in the joy of the expectant or new parents. If you've been selected as the host, consider it an honor to gather everyone together to shower the baby with gifts and best wishes. You've been entrusted with this very special event and the best gift you can give mom, or mom-to-be, is a unique and unforgettable baby shower. While the basic ingredients for a baby shower are the refreshments, activities and gift opening, you can add a heaping measure of fun with all-new, creative games for your guests to enjoy.

Your guests will be pleasantly surprised when you introduce contemporary games that are fun and easy to learn. Imagine their delight when you play a baby shower game they've never seen before. These brand new games will be met with enthusiasm and the excitement will overflow into the festivities making it a joyous occasion for all who attend.

# HOW TO BENEFIT THE MOST FROM THIS BOOK

I suggest you take a moment to read the definitions of the following steps for each game and activity. The step-by-step instructions are provided to help you host the games and activities with ease.

## Materials Needed

A complete list of everything you need will help you determine if you can add the game or activity to your shower based on the cost and availability of materials needed.

## Preparation (Before the shower)

What you need to do before the day of the shower to make the craft activities ready to make or the games ready to play.

To make game hosting easier place the supplies, prizes and favors for each game or activity in a large paper grocery bag and label it with the title of the game or activity. During the shower you'll have everything you need ready to go and right at your fingertips.

## Preparation (Before you begin)

What you need to do before the guests begin the craft activity at the shower.

## Preparation (Before you play)

What you need to do before the guests start to play the game at the shower.

## Introducing the Game

Setting the scene for the game will delight the guests and bring their attention to your announcement for the rules on how to play.

**How to Play**

After you captivate your audience with the brief storytelling introduction, explain the rules for how to play the game. If you'd like to demonstrate the game with a practice run, it will help the guests visualize the object of the game. Their enthusiasm for the games and activities will be greater when they know exactly what needs to be done.

**Prizes and Favors**

Keep in mind these are only suggestions to suit the theme of the game or activity. Choose what you can easily afford or have available.

Have extra prizes and favors on hand for the following reasons: Some guests may bring a friend or relative. Not everyone remembers to RSVP. Extra prizes are great in case of a tie and it's always better to have too many than not enough.

If you have a prize or two leftover at the end of the shower, present them to your helpers at the event. Did someone share in the planning and preparation for the shower, take pictures for you, help with serving the guests or assist with the games? Award them with a small token and a big "Thank You" to express your appreciation.

**Chapters**

Pages 4 through 6 outline the chapters and give a brief description of each category based on the types of games or activities included in the chapter. This is especially useful when planning the games for your shower. You wouldn't want to select all tossing games as it would take too much time for everyone to take a turn. A shower filled with relays would have your guests worn out before the gift-opening portion of the shower. Dividing the games into categories allows you to select one or two from each chapter for a good combination of active and quiet games.

**Page Headings**

The page numbers along with the chapter headings at the top of each page will make it easier for you to find each category of games and activities.

# *Arrival Activities*

Although you've designated a start time for the shower to begin, not all of your guests will arrive on time. Welcome the guests with an activity as they arrive. While you accept the gift and escort each guest to the party area, present the materials needed and announce the simple instructions for the arrival "icebreaker" activity.

The new arrival will feel at ease with a fun project and the other guests can assist if needed. This opening activity will serve as an icebreaker and allow you the opportunity to greet the other guests as they arrive.

# *Relays*

Before you add a "running" relay race to your game line-up, consider these factors: Is there enough space on carpeting or lawn to run the relay and will your guests be willing to endure a "marathon." More conservative shower attendees may not be willing to kick off their heels and run around the yard while younger guests may find it a welcome change of pace. Keep in mind not all may wish to participate in a running relay so some of the relays in this chapter are "seated" relays for the guests you know best.

### *Running Relay*

Requires two equal teams and two turnaround points. If the teams are uneven, ask a participant to run the race twice. Turnaround points can be any of the following: Plastic trash cans, chairs, empty boxes, a person or any two items that are similar and safe. Make sure they are spaced evenly from the start line and far enough apart to avoid opposing team member collisions. For relay races on lawn choose an area that is free from sprinklers, sticks or other dangerous objects. Relay races can be exciting and fun, but they can also be dangerous if not well planned and properly supervised.

### *Seated Relay*

Requires two equal teams lined up and seated in evenly spaced rows.

## *Everybody Wins*

It's amazing how something as innocent as a baby shower can bring out the competitive edge in everyone, even the most mild-mannered guest may surprise you. I've personally witnessed the simple game of "Can't Say Baby" nearly ruin several baby showers I've attended. To calm everyone's competitive spirit, why not introduce a game where everyone's a winner.

## *Tossing Games*

Tossing games, like the ones played at carnivals, are a favorite at parties. With all of the brain-teasing games presented at most showers, these games requiring only a quick flick of the wrist are a welcome addition to the line-up of activities. Everyone will enjoy the opportunity to stretch their legs and test their tossing skills in these baby themed games. Always hold a toss-off or award all tie winners. Selecting a number from 1 to 10 as a tiebreaker isn't nearly as exciting as a rematch.

## *Circle Games*

Provide a balance in your baby shower game plan by alternating active (relays, tossing and action games) and quiet games (arrival activities, circle and ready-to-copy games). Add a circle game immediately following an active game to set the pace for a variety of fun-filled activities.

## *Active Games*

Alternating active and quiet games is a very good idea for any occasion. These exciting and lively games were designed to complement a well-balanced schedule of activities.

## *Traditional Games*

Although everyone typically gags at the thought of tasting baby food, dislikes the idea of being told "what not to say" and can't stand the brain-teasing of another paper challenge, you know everyone still has their favorite games when it comes to attending showers. For those of you who would like to include an old (or new) favorite for nostalgia's sake, this list of traditional games will remind you of games from shower's past.

## *Ready to Copy Games*

"Ready to Copy" games are ideal for any baby shower. All you have to do is make the copies before the party and hand them out with pencils or pens at game time. Be sure to select enough prizes in case of a tie or have an extra game planned as a tiebreaker.

## *Door Prizes*

Who doesn't enjoy a raffle, lottery or door prize drawing? It's a chance for the guests without the baby shower game skills to actually have an opportunity to win something at the party. This chapter is filled with new ideas for awarding a prize to a guest just for attending and sharing in the best wishes for the new baby.

# TIPS FOR GAME PLANNING

## Making a Schedule

The ideal baby shower schedule includes an arrival activity, games, refreshments, gift opening and a farewell activity (door prize). If you want your party to last 2 hours plan on a 15 minute arrival activity, 45 minutes of games, refreshments for 30 minutes and the gift opening for 30 minutes. Close the shower with a door prize giveaway and you can easily fill a 2-hour period.

What if things don't go according to my plan? This is true of almost every party I've hosted or attended. It's extremely important to be relaxed and willing to change your schedule to accommodate your guests. The schedule is only an outline to help you manage the shower with ease. Flexibility is the key to ensure it's success.

## Selecting Games and Activities

The most important thing to remember when selecting games and activities for a celebration is to include the guest of honor. Who knows best which games will be the hit of the party? Your mom, or mom-to-be, will know the personalities of the attendees and which games and activities will be met with enthusiasm. Make a preliminary list of the games you can do based on availability and cost of materials. Review some of the games with your guest of honor and choose their favorites. Surprises are nice, so now that you know the types of games she prefers, pick 1 or 2 more and add them to the line-up.

## Selecting Games and Activities for a Surprise Shower

If you are planning a surprise shower, use their hobbies and favorite things as a guide when making your selections. If she is a scrapbooking addict, introduce "Welcome Mats" as the arrival activity and "Brag Books" for the door prize giveaway. You know she's creative, so select more games that inspire creativity to fill the rest of your line-up. If she is very athletic and full of energy, be sure to include "Baby Bottle Bowling" and "Baseball or Ballet." Ask a mutual friend or two if they agree with your selections and to contribute their own ideas.

# TIPS FOR GAME PLANNING

### How Many Games Should We Play?

Remember the baby showers you attended in the past where the host would play every game in the book? Well, you can't do that with this book or your shower will turn into a sleepover.

Select only one arrival activity for the start of your shower and one door prize giveaway for the end of your shower. Review the list of the games you would like to play and make an actual game plan for the games and activities that will fill the game portion of your schedule (approximately 45 minutes).

Most of the games average 5 to 10 minutes for a shower consisting of up to 12 guests. Select 4 to 6 games and two extras. Be sure to select games from different chapters so you can vary the times for play. This will typically bring you very close to 45 minutes. Let your guest's enthusiasm be your guide. If they are enjoying the games, keep playing. If they look like they are ready to take a break for refreshments, play only 4 or 5 games. Remember, flexibility is the key to your shower's success.

If you have a very large guest list, consisting of 15 or more attendees, play only 3 or 4 games. The game times will be extended and the gift-opening portion of the shower will take much longer. Shortening the game plan will keep the party from running into overtime.

### The Game Plan

Write down the order in which you would like to play the games. It's a good idea to follow up a relay or active game with a quiet game or activity. By alternating active and quiet games you can maintain a balance in the energy levels of your guests and keep the party manageable.

### Rainy Day Plan

No one can predict what Mother Nature will do on the day of your shower, so it's always best to have an indoor plan. Most of the games in this book can be played in or out of doors. If you've selected a few games or relays that can only be played outside, choose and prepare a few alternate games for a rainy day plan.

# TIPS FOR GAME HOSTING

## A Little Help From Your Friends and Relatives

Call upon a friend or relative to assist you at the shower to help you with the games and activities, serving refreshments, gift opening and clean up. Assign the duties each of you will be responsible for during the shower. Remember to show your appreciation by sending a thank you card, inviting them to lunch or by offering to return the favor at their next party.

Teenagers are great party assistants. They gladly accept fun, money-making opportunities. Offer to pay more than a babysitter's regular fee; it will be a good investment. Clearly define what their duties will be throughout the shower.

## Siblings

Older siblings (ages 8 and up) will feel special on this day if you allow them to help with the games and activities. They can help you set up the games and assist the guests as they arrive with the craft activities. They can retrieve the items tossed in the carnival style games. If a relay calls for an even numbered player, they can fill in the space. Assign them the duty of "prize monitor" to hand out the prizes and favors for each game.

Helping with the games is more fun than a chore. They'll be delighted with the responsibility and feel as though they contributed to the success of the shower. Be sure to award them a special prize for their assistance.

## Candid Moments

Ask an "aspiring" amateur photographer to take pictures during the games (a friend, neighbor or relative). Game participants are the best models when they're too busy having fun to notice the camera. You'll have some great candid shots to add to the memory book for the shower.

## Safety Tip

Be careful with small game and activity materials or food items that may present a choking hazard. Keep out of reach if near infants, toddlers or pets.

# BABY SHOWER THEMES

Should you decide to choose a theme, the ideas for your baby shower will begin to pour. Here are some suggestions to help with the brainstorm.

### *Creative Minds*
Little Bloomers
Decorate the Nursery
Quilting Bee
Scrapbooking

### *Party Animals*
Circus
Noah's Ark
Zoo
Safari

### *Menu Makers*
Luau
Potluck
Picnic
Tea Party
Pickles and "Ice Cream Social"

### *Dress It Up*
A Star is Born
1950's
Storybook Character
Nursery Rhymes
Cowgirl/Cowboy

# BABY SHOWER THEMES

Should you decide to choose a theme, the ideas for your baby shower will begin to pour. Here are some more suggestions to help with the brainstorm.

### *It's a Boy*
Blue
Sports
"Under" Construction
Dinosaurs

### *It's a Girl*
Pink
Princess
Butterflies
Ballerina

### *Holidays*
Valentine
St. Patrick's Day
Easter
Halloween
Thanksgiving
Christmas

### *Baby Things*
Teddy Bears
Stork
Umbrellas
ABC's (block)
Rubber Duckies
Rocking Horse

# BABY SHOWER INVITATIONS

Make a list of the friends and family the guest of honor would like to attend. If this is a surprise shower, ask more than one friend or family member for the names of those who should be included. Be sure to write down the address and phone number of each guest.

You and the guest of honor should determine the best date and time to have the shower. It is not recommended to select a date within four to five weeks of the due date, either before or after, as babies can be very unpredictable when it comes to time of delivery and you may have to reschedule. Six to eight weeks before the due date is ideal as mom-to-be is not as uncomfortable as she would be in the last weeks of pregnancy, it allows time to prepare the nursery with the new gifts and she will be able to send out her thank you notes before the arrival. If the celebration is to be after the baby is born, allow four to six weeks for mom to settle in to her new baby's schedule before you actually set the date.

Three to four weeks before the date of the shower is when the invitations should be mailed. Although you do request an RSVP (abbreviation for a French expression which means "please reply"), all you invite may not remember to respond. It is acceptable for you to graciously call upon the guests to see if they will be in attendance and to offer any information they may need. This will give you an accurate number of attendees so you may plan the refreshments and games for the baby shower.

# BABY SHOWER DECORATIONS

Hosting a baby shower requires taking on the role of interior decorator. Decorating is your opportunity to be creative in showering the guests with a festive environment. The streamers, balloons, centerpieces and tableware will be needed for the basic scene setters but you can add your own special and unique touches, as well.

If you have selected a theme for the baby shower, decorate the room with stuffed animals, toys and items related to your theme. Baby toys and baby care products are wonderful decorations if you do not have a specific theme. These items can be presented to the mom, or mom-to-be, after the shower as an added surprise. Flowers and fruit are beautiful when used as centerpieces. I'm sure you've seen the very popular watermelon baby carriage at a previous celebration or beautiful flower bouquets on display.

# GIFT IDEAS

The inclusion of gift registry information in a shower invitation has become very popular. Be sure to ask the parents if they wish to register for gifts or if they would like the gifts from friends and family to be a surprise. For the gift registry to be a success, you must decide early and have the guest of honor register at the store before the invitations are mailed.

As the hostess, most of your time and budget will be spent on the baby shower. With a little creativity, you can present an affordable gift that can also be displayed as a decorative centerpiece. A beautiful basket filled with baby necessities, a bathtub overflowing with bathing accessories or a set of baby bottles filled with candy as a special treat for the parents-to-be.

# SIMPLE SERVING SUGGESTIONS

## Keep it Simple

Hosting a baby shower also requires taking on the role of caterer. In order for your shower to be a success, keep it simple so you may enjoy the celebration, as well. By serving simple, self-serve refreshments you provide a variety of food and beverages to please everyone in attendance. You may serve a meal if you wish, although most guests will truly appreciate a brunch style buffet of finger foods and nonalcoholic beverages.

## When to Serve Refreshments

According to the game planning tip "Making a Schedule" on page 7, it is best to serve the refreshments immediately after the games are played. The guests will be ready to enjoy beverages, snacks, conversation and relaxation after the spirit of competition. If you will be serving only dessert at your shower, this would be the best time to cut the cake. When it appears everyone has been served and is nearly finished with their refreshments, it will be time to open the gifts.

If you are serving a meal at the shower, some prefer to save the cake until after the gift opening portion of the shower. Please do keep in mind that offering the cake at the end of the shower will leave it open to when guests feel they are expected to leave. By serving the cake before the gifts, the opening of the gifts signifies the end of the shower and guests will be more inclined to depart. This is especially important to mom who needs to care for baby, or for mom-to-be who may appreciate a little rest being so near her due date.

If you would like to serve the cake at the end of the shower, announce a door prize giveaway after everyone has finished eating dessert. Awarding the door prize and thanking everyone for attending will signify the end of the shower.

# SIMPLE SERVING SUGGESTIONS

## Beverages

As the hostess, you will have enough to manage at the shower without having to monitor alcohol consumption. While most friends and relatives can drink responsibly, alcohol will add an extra level of concern for those who may have a little too much to drink. Not only could the results disrupt the shower, but arranging for their transportation home will also add to your duties. It is perfectly acceptable to offer only nonalcoholic beverages at the baby shower. With the guest of honor either pregnant or nursing baby it has become the standard at most showers to serve only nonalcoholic beverages.

Large, decorative buckets filled with ice to keep the beverages cold make it easy for guests to serve themselves. The bottles and cans also prevent as many spills from occurring. If you would like to serve sherbet punch (a traditional favorite at baby showers), be sure to use heavyweight paper cups that won't easily tip over. If you will be serving coffee, use heavyweight mugs to avoid hot spills.

## Finger Foods or a Meal?

There are ways to make simple finger foods seem elegant without cutting into your budget or time. Fancy garnishments, unique serving trays and beautiful table décor can enhance any buffet. Finger sandwiches, cold cut tortilla wraps, cheese and crackers, chips and dip, fresh fruits and raw vegetables are favorites at any gathering.

If you would like to serve a meal, why not consider a taco or baked potato bar. Guests can serve themselves and the toppings are easy to prepare in advance. Side dishes for a taco bar; spanish rice, beans and chips and salsa. For a potato bar; steamed vegetables, chili and pizza toppings.

Party supply stores have a wide variety of baby shower tableware, such as paper plates, cups, napkins, table covers and centerpieces to help make presentation and serving festive and the clean up a lot easier.

# BABY ANNOUNCEMENTS

### Materials Needed

1 piece of paper or cardstock per guest
1 pen or marking pen per guest
color pencils or marking pens

### Preparation

Before the shower – fold each paper in half to resemble a greeting card.

Before you begin – give one piece of folded paper and one pen to each guest. Supply color pencils or marking pens for everyone to share.

### How to Make

Ask everyone to design a greeting card announcement for the new baby (or baby-to-be). Here are two examples: "We're thinking pink for our new baby girl" and "We have a brand new bundle of boy." After each guest designs and colors their announcement, collect the papers for the guest of honor to share and keep as a remembrance. The guest of honor may wish to select a favorite to copy and send as baby's official announcement. Be sure to give credit to the designer on the card.

**Tip:** If the shower is to welcome baby, design a "thank you" note instead.

# BABYSITTING CLUB

## Materials Needed

1 index or note card per guest
1 pen per guest

## Preparation

Before the shower – none.

Before you begin – give one index or note card and one pen to each guest.

## How to Make

In a few short sentences, write a funny, charming or most memorable babysitting experience. Collect the short stories and save the cards for later in the shower. While the guests are relaxing and enjoying their refreshments, the hostess of the party will read them aloud to share the memories with everyone.

## Door Prize Option

Award a prize for the funniest or most heartwarming story.

# CHARMING BRACELETS

## Materials Needed

10 inches of elastic string per guest
several bulk packages of beads and charms
  (optional: pink if "it's a girl", blue if "it's a boy")
1 diaper pin per guest
1 reclosable sandwich bag per guest
safety scissors

## Preparation

Before the shower – design a sample bracelet to determine how many beads and charms would make a charming bracelet for each guest. Place an elastic string tied to the closed end of a diaper pin and the correct number of beads and charms in a reclosable sandwich bag for each guest. The diaper pin will keep the beads in place while creating the charming bracelet.

Before you begin – give each guest one bag filled with everything they need to design a charming bracelet.

## How to Make

Announce the bracelet is a party favor to take home, so be sure to size the bracelet to fit the person it will adorn. When the beads and charms are in place and sized to fit, tie off the ends and trim the excess string.

# DIAPER ORIGAMI

## Materials Needed

1 square piece of white paper per guest
  (trim 8 ½" x 11" to 8 ½" x 8 ½")

## Preparation

Before the shower – for each guest, trim a piece of paper to a square size.

Before you begin – give each guest a piece of plain white paper, "a diaper," when they arrive.

## How to Make

Explain Diaper Origami is any creative folding technique they wish to invent to fashion a "gift" for the baby. Present all of the gifts to the mom or mom-to-be.

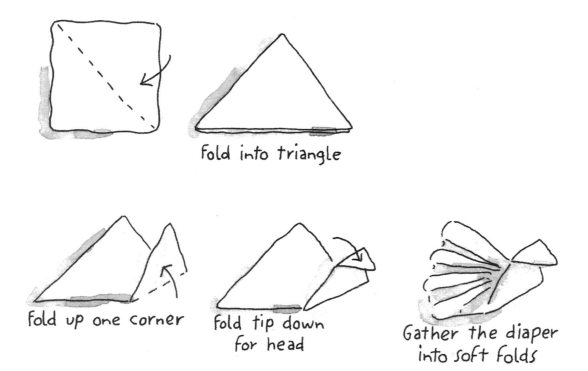

Fold into triangle

Fold up one corner

Fold tip down for head

Gather the diaper into soft folds

# MINI MOBILES

## Materials Needed

1 small (child size) plastic hanger per guest
5 chenille stems per guest

## Preparation

Before the shower – none.

Before you begin – give each guest one plastic hanger and 5 chenille stems.

## How to Make

Invite the guests to build a "mini mobile" using items from their purse. If a guest did not bring their purse to the shower, they can team with another guest and build the mobile together. Award a prize for one of these categories: most practical, prettiest, baby safe or most unusual.

Each guest will keep her own "mini mobile" work of art. Photograph the prizewinning mini mobiles for a special memory.

# QUILTING BEE

**Materials Needed**

1 square piece of paper per guest (3" x 3", 4" x 4" or 5" x 5")
color marking pens
crayons
stickers
glue and miscellaneous craft supplies

**Preparation**

Before the shower – count the RSVP's to make sure you will have enough guests to complete a square quilt. Should it not add up to an even quilt, decorate a few extra squares to fill in the spaces. For numerous attendees, you may wish to use smaller squares for a manageable mural.

Before you begin – give each guest a square piece of paper. Supply color marking pens, crayons, stickers and craft supplies for the guests to share.

**How to Make**

Invite each guest to create a patchwork quilt square for the baby with designs and/or their best wishes. Before the end of the shower, tape the squares together to resemble a patchwork quilt and lay the designer quilt on the table for all to see. Present to the guest of honor as a keepsake mural.

 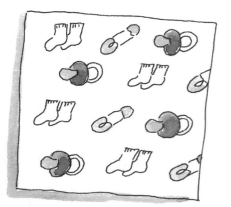

# WELCOME MATS

## Materials Needed

1 picture frame mat board per guest
color marking pens
stickers
craft supplies

## Preparation

Before the shower – none.

Before you begin – give one mat board frame to each guest upon arrival. Supply color marking pens, stickers and craft supplies for the guests to share.

## How to Make

Invite the guests to decorate their "welcome-the-baby" mats. Mom will have many photo opportunities in the years to come. Each handmade frame can display baby's best photos in a true "work of heart" designed by family and friends.

# WHO AM I?

## Materials Needed

1 self-adhesive name badge per guest
1 black marking pen
color marking pens
stickers

## Preparation

Before the shower – with a black marking pen, write in the center of each blank name badge the guest's first name. Make one badge per guest.

Before you begin – give each guest his or her own personalized name badge. Supply marking pens and stickers for the guests to decorate their badge.

## How to Make

Announce to each guest as they pick up their name badge to create designs that reflect their own personality, children, career, hobbies or how they know the guest of honor. After the badges are complete and in place, everyone can greet one another to introduce themselves and have a head start on getting to know the other guests. The designs on the name badges will intrigue the other guests to inquire about their meanings.

# BEDTIME STORY RELAY

### Materials Needed

2 picture storybooks
  (do not use titles that are keepsakes)

### Preparation

Before the shower – none.

Before you play – set up the turnaround
points and divide the guests into two teams.

### Introducing the Relay

"It's a race to see who gets to read
  the first bedtime story to baby."

### How to Play

Place the storybook on top of the head of the first runner for each team. The
first runner must circle the turnaround point while balancing the book during
the entire course of the relay. Return to the line and place the book on the
next runner's head. The first team to "keep their storybook balance" and
finish the relay wins.

**Prizes:** Miniature storybooks.

# BOTTLE WARMERS

## Materials Needed

2 plastic baby bottles, same size
4 oven mitts
1 cotton ball per guest

## Preparation

Before the shower – none.

Before you play – divide the guests into two teams. Everyone is to be seated in this relay. Designate the first player for each team by supplying one cotton ball, one plastic bottle and two oven mitts to the starting player on each team. Give one cotton ball to each of the remaining players on both teams.

## Introducing the Relay

"Because we must always test the temperature of baby's formula, use these oven mitts in case it's too hot to handle."

## How to Play

The first player begins the relay by putting on the oven mitts, twisting off the lid and placing the cotton ball into the baby bottle. Put the lid back on the bottle and pass the bottle and the oven mitts to the next player to continue the relay. Each player must twist off the cap, add their cotton ball to the bottle while wearing the oven mitts, replace the lid and pass it on to the next player. First team to fill their bottle with cotton balls wins the relay.

**Prizes:** "Cool" refrigerator magnets.

# CAR POOL RELAY

## Materials Needed

1 stuffed animal or doll per guest
2 laundry baskets

## Preparation

Before the shower – none.

Before you play – set up laundry
baskets filled with an even number
of stuffed animals and dolls as the
turnaround points. Divide the guests
into two teams.

## Introducing the Relay

"With a new baby, soon it will be your turn to pick up everybody in the car
pool, Brandon at baseball, Sarah at soccer, Mattie at the vet. You will need
to designate more drivers."

## How to Play

The first runner will begin the relay by running to the laundry basket to pick
up one passenger (stuffed animal or doll), bring it back to the next player in
line. Player number two must carry the first runner's passenger, while they
go to pick up another passenger from the basket. When player number two
returns to the starting point, player number three will be carrying both
passengers to go pick up one more. Sounds like a real-life chaotic car pool!
Continue handing off passengers until the last player is carrying all of the
passengers and makes it back to the starting point without dropping (off) any
of the "children or pets." The first team to finish the car pool relay wins.

**Prizes:** Small toy cars.

# DIRTY DIAPER RELAY

## Materials Needed

2 disposable diapers

## Preparation

Before the shower – none.

Before you play – Pour a small measure of water into each diaper to make it full, fold and seal with the adhesive closures. Set up the turnaround points and divide the guests into two teams. Supply a "dirty" diaper to the first runner on each team.

## Introducing the Relay

"It's hands off dirty diapers as you pass diaper duty onto your teammate."

## How to Play

The first runner will decide how they wish to carry the diaper to the turnaround point, *no hands!* They can hold inside of elbow, under chin, between the knees or anyway they can carry without actually touching the diaper with their hands. The first runner must circle the turnaround point and pass the dirty diaper to the next runner without using their hands. When they have accomplished the "hand-off," the race continues. If a dirty diaper is dropped during the course of the relay, it must be picked up at the point where it fell, placed where it was carried and the race continued. The first team to finish the relay wins.

**Prizes:** Air fresheners for car or home that are fun or fancy.

# PIGGY BANK RELAY

### Materials Needed

2 piggy banks (break resistant)
   If you don't have two piggy banks,
   design banks with empty butter tubs
   by cutting slots into the lids and
   decorating with baby gift wrapping paper.

### Preparation

Before the shower – none.

Before you play – divide the guests into two teams. Everyone is to be seated in this relay. Supply a piggy bank to the starting player on each team.

### Introducing the Relay

"College is so expensive, let's start saving for baby now."

### How to Play

Announce each guest will contribute five coins to the piggy bank as it is passed down the line. No searching for the coins will be allowed until the relay begins. This will make the relay more frantic as the guests try to find the coins in the bottom of their purses or pockets. If a player is broke, they can borrow coins from another team member. The starting player can begin the relay with the first five coins. Pass the bank to the next player and continue until the relay is complete. After the relay, count the money in each piggy bank. The winning team is not the one who finishes first, but the team that was more generous (with the most money in their bank).

Give the guest of honor the banks with the money inside as a head start on college tuition for the new baby.

**Prizes:** Coin purses.

# SOAP BOX DUCKIE

## Materials Needed

1 bar of soap (in the box) per guest
1 rubber duck per guest
1 kitchen table or counter
   (smooth surface)

## Preparation

Before the shower – none.

Before you play – give each guest
one bar of soap and one rubber duck.

## Introducing the Relay

"The race is on to see who can build a better soap box racer for baby."

## How to Play

There will be two challengers at a time (if you have a large number of guests, race three at a time). Line up the first two guests on the same side of the table. The duck will be sitting on top of the box to begin the race. Each guest will push off the soap box duckie from the designated starting line (the closest end of the table). The soap box racer that slides the farthest distance without losing the rubber duck wins the race and is able to compete in the next round. Keep racing until you have a winner in the final round.

## Party Favor Suggestion

Everyone keeps the soap and the rubber duck "soap box racer" as a favor.

**Prizes:** Trophy or first place ribbon.

# STORK RELAY

## Materials Needed

2 hard-boiled eggs
2 bandannas or handkerchiefs

## Preparation

Before the shower – hard boil 6 to 8 eggs and cool (some may crack while boiling, keep extras for the day of the shower). Fashion and tie two bandannas to resemble a stork's baby carrier.

Before you play – set up the turnaround points and divide the guests into two teams. Supply an egg bundled in a bandanna to the first runner on each team.

## Introducing the Relay

"You're carrying a very precious cargo, don't drop this special delivery."

## How to Play

The first runner will carry the egg within the bandanna or handkerchief to the turnaround point, return to their team and hand off the "special delivery" to the next player. Continue until the first team to carefully complete the relay without dropping the egg wins.

## Game Tip

For an added surprise, if you are playing this game outdoors, use a raw egg. The team who drops the delivery will, without a doubt, forfeit the relay.

**Prizes:** Handkerchiefs or bandannas.

# TWINKLE, TWINKLE LITTLE STAR

## Materials Needed

2 sheets of pink, blue or yellow construction paper per 4 guests
scissors
1 marking pen
2 large envelopes or lunch bags

## Preparation

Before the shower – cut the star shapes from the construction paper and write the guests names on the stars, one guest per star. Make two sets of star cut-outs, one set for each envelope. For example: If you have 12 guests, envelope #1 will contain 12 stars, one named per guest and envelope #2 will contain 12 stars with one named per guest, as well.

Before you play – divide the guests into two teams. Everyone is to remain seated in this relay. Give the starting player on each team an envelope containing star cut-outs named after each guest in attendance.

## Introducing the Relay

"Twinkle, Twinkle Little Star, how I wonder what you are…."

## How to Play

The starting player will reach for the stars by looking in the envelope to find his or her star. The guest will keep the star with their name written on it and return all of the remaining stars to the envelope and hand off to the next player on the team to continue the relay. Each guest must retrieve his or her own star. The first team to collect their personalized stars will win the relay.

**Name Tag Option:** Hand out safety pins and use the stars as name tags.

**Door Prize Option:** Combine the stars remaining in the team's envelopes (there will be one per guest). Reach in and draw one star as the winner of a door prize.

# BABY RINGS, STRINGS AND THINGS

## Materials Needed

1 diaper pail
1 baby ring (inexpensive wedding party favor rings) per guest
1 spool of yarn (choose a pastel "baby" color)
1 prize per guest
white gift wrapping paper
scissors
tape

## Preparation

Before the shower – cut a one yard length of yarn per guest. Tape each string of yarn to an individually wrapped prize. Then tie the other end of the string to a party favor ring. Place all of the prizes into a diaper pail with a lid. Allow the string (yarn) from each gift to hang outside of the container. Only the rings with a portion of each individual string will be visible.

Before you play – none.

## Introducing the Game

"These strings are attached in this diaper-filled pail, pull on one for a diaper full of fun."

## How to Play

Each guest will take a turn to select and pull on one string to retrieve a prize from inside the diaper pail.

**Game Tip:** For a gag gift, wrap a "dirty" diaper as a prize. Smear melted chocolate into a disposable diaper and fold to wrap as a prize. When the unsuspecting guest opens the "surprise diaper" award an extra special gift to the good sport. Be sure to announce it's a "sweet surprise" of chocolate.

# BARGAIN HUNTERS

## Materials Needed

1 baby or parenting magazine
   per guest
   (a local free parenting
   publication would be
   very inexpensive)

## Preparation

Before the shower – be sure
the magazines are exactly
the same issue for each
guest. Choose 3 or 4 items
(product advertisements)
and list them along with
their page numbers for
your reference only.

Before you play – hand out one magazine to each guest.

## Introducing the Game

"Let's learn the basics of bargain hunting 101."

## How to Play

Announce the first item (or product) to hunt. The guests are not allowed to open their magazines until you say "ready, set, shop." Then each guest will try to locate the page number where the item appears. The first person to yell out the page number is the winner. Close the magazines and announce another item for everyone to play again.

**Prizes:** Newsstand magazines (entertainment, home décor, fashion, etc.). Everyone keeps the baby or parenting magazine as a party favor.

# DIAPER WRAPS

## Materials Needed

1 disposable diaper per guest
1 prize per guest

## Preparation

Before the shower – wrap one prize in a disposable diaper per guest.

Before you play – hand out one diaper filled with a prize to each guest and ask the guests to pair off in teams of two each.

## Introducing the Game

"These diapers are actually filled with pleasant surprises. Your duty is to guess what's inside the diaper."

## How to Play

Announce to the guests to peek inside their surprise filled diaper and then exchange it with their teammate. Each guest will ask his or her teammate to feel the prize through the diaper and guess what the prize is. If the teammate can't guess the item, the one who knows what's inside can give a clue or two until the teammate guesses and wins the prize they are holding. Now it's time for the other guest to guess what's inside the diaper.

**Prizes:** Fun items to include would be breath mints or candies in unique packaging, key chains, play putty, small toys, brush or anything small enough to fit in a disposable diaper. Browse the aisles at the dollar stores for more ideas. Do not select anything breakable.

# NEST EGGS

## Materials Needed

1 plastic fill egg (save from Easter) per guest
2 or more pieces of play paper money of various dollar amounts per guest
1 party favor per guest
1 large package of individually wrapped candies
1 "nest" basket

## Preparation

Before the shower – fill each egg with play money, wrapped candies and a party favor. Make sure one of the eggs has the largest amount of money compared to the other eggs. Fill the "nest" basket with eggs and display as a centerpiece for the shower.

Before you play – Pass the basket around the room so each guest may select one nest egg to crack open.

## Introducing the Game

"Who saved the most for this rainy day, baby's shower."

## How to Play

Each guest will count the contents of their egg to see who has the most money put away in the "nest egg." The winner of the game is the guest with the highest dollar amount.

**Prizes:** Everyone keeps their party favor filled "nest egg" as a prize.

# PASS THE PRESENTS

## Materials Needed

1 prize per guest
gift wrapping paper
scissors and tape
music

## Preparation

Before the shower – wrap one present per guest.

Before you play – hand out one wrapped present to each guest.

## Introducing the Game

"Returns and exchanges can be quite a chore, when you can't decide which gift you like more."

## How to Play

Play music (a lullaby or baby song) for two or three minutes while the guests pass the presents. Each guest will pass a present to the next guest and continue until the music stops. Each guest is allowed to have only one gift in his or her hands at all times. Some guests might like what they're holding and slow down the game intentionally, while others may pick up the pace to get their hands on a more desirable (or bigger) gift. When the music stops, ask which guests would like to keep their gift and bow out of the next round. Play up to three rounds. On the final round, everyone must keep the gift that falls into his or her own hands. No exchanges or refunds.

**Game Tip:** Prizes of various shapes, sizes and sounds will make the game more fun to play and watch as everyone tries to figure out what's inside as they pass it along.

**Prizes:** Puzzles, wooden spoon set, candy tin, candle, sunglasses, sachets.

# PICKLES AND ICE CREAM

## Materials Needed

1 empty ice cream container (rinse and dry)
1 prize per guest
paper
pencil
scissors

## Preparation

Before the shower – cut the paper into squares, two per guest. Write down one main course, junk food or dessert item on each slip of paper. If you have 12 guests, you will need 24 slips of paper with one food item listed on each piece of paper. Items that could upset your stomach if combined will work best: chili, sushi, pizza, kraut dog, quiche, beef jerky, peanut butter pretzels, spinach, pudding, fruitcake, etc. Fold the papers and place them in the ice cream container.

Before you play – none.

## Introducing the Game

"Mom's-to-be have some crazy cravings when it comes to food, help her think of some new combinations for some belly-aching laughs."

## How to Play

Each guest is to select two pieces of paper from the ice cream container. After everyone has their new crazy cravings combination, call upon each guest to announce the new prizewinning pair of food items. Pickles and ice cream will probably sound a lot more appetizing at the end of this game. Award a prize to everyone for suggesting a new crazy craving.

**Prizes:** Ice cream gift certificates.

# PUZZLE PRIZES

### Materials Needed

1 copy of a baby picture per guest
  (pictures of a famous baby,
    the new baby or mom-to-be's
    baby photo)
1 envelope per guest
1 prize per guest
1 marking pen
1 pencil
scissors
tape

### Preparation

Before the shower – reprint a favorite baby photo or copy a baby picture, one for each guest. On the back of each picture write the name of one prize in large, bold letters with the marking pen. Draw a simple jigsaw puzzle pattern on the back of each picture in pencil. Cut the pattern into pieces and insert the puzzle into an envelope and seal. You will need one puzzle per envelope, per guest.

Before you play – hand out one envelope containing a puzzle to each guest.

### Introducing the Game

"Piece together a puzzle to discover a prizewinning baby photo."

### How to Play

Ask the guests to open their envelopes and put together the puzzle inside. When it's complete, use only enough transparent tape to hold the pieces in place. Have the guests turn over their completed puzzle to reveal the name of the prize written on the back. Award the prizes accordingly.

**Prizes:** Miniature puzzles, brag books, picture frames and magnet frames.

# SPIN THE BABY BOTTLE

## Materials Needed

1 baby bottle
water
1 prize per guest

## Preparation

Before the shower – fill the baby
bottle with a small measure of
water for a better balance in spinning.

Before you play – form a circle with
the prizes and position the baby bottle
on its side in the center of the prizes.

## Introducing the Game

"When you spin this bottle you won't get a kiss, but it's still a game you
won't want to miss."

## How to Play

Each guest will take one turn to spin the bottle. The prize the nipple points to
is the prize the guest will get to keep. If it falls in the middle of two prizes,
spin again. Close in the circle of prizes as they are won and continue to play
until every guest has won a prize.

**Prizes:** Mugs, toothpick holders, salt & pepper shakers, measuring spoons,
recipe cards, oven mitts, inexpensive kitchen items.

# DIRTY DIAPERS

## Materials Needed

1 diaper pail
1 package of disposable diapers
1 marking pen

## Preparation

Before the shower – none.

Before you play – place a diaper pail in the middle of the room. Open a package of disposable diapers and as you give one to each guest, write their first name on the outside of the diaper with the marking pen.

## Introducing the Game

"Dispose of these dirty diapers as fast as you can."

## How to Play

Everyone will stand and toss their diaper into the pail at once. The diapers that landed in the pail are handed out to the winners, according to the names written on them, for round two and so on. Continue to toss off until only one winner is left standing.

**Prizes:**  Box of chocolates.

# IT'S A DATE

## Materials Needed

1 large wall calendar
1 penny
paper and pencil

## Preparation

Before the shower – list the guest's names on a piece of paper.

Before you play – open the calendar to the birth month, or expected birth month, of the baby and place it on the floor. Designate a throw line and have the guests form a single file line behind it.

## Introducing the Game

"Let's pool our pennies and pitch a date for baby's arrival."

## How to Play

Each guest will have a turn to toss a penny at the calendar on the floor. Record each guest's toss by listing the date of the square the penny lands in next to the name. The guest who lands directly on, or closest to, baby's due date or birth date wins.

**Prizes:** Calendar or appointment book.

# MINI-STORAGE

## Materials Needed

1 empty plastic diaper wipe container
1 package of clothespins or blocks

## Preparation

Before the shower – none.

Before you play – set up the diaper wipe container as a target. Designate a throw line and have the guests form a single file line behind it.

## Introducing the Game

"Make a mini-storage unit by tossing items in to recycle diaper wipe bins."

## How to Play

Each guest will have a turn to toss 6 clothespins or blocks into the diaper wipe container. The guest with the most successes wins. In case of a tie, play additional rounds to determine a winner.

**Prizes:** Mini-storage units (decorative baskets or bins for keepsakes, etc.)

## Mini-Storage Tip

Diaper wipe containers with lids are great for storing items to keep at your fingertips; first aid kit, sewing supplies, batteries, baby socks, make-up, travel size needs, mini-building blocks, doll accessories, etc.

# NURSERY RHYME TOSS

**Materials Needed**

"Little Miss Muffet"
3 plastic toy spiders
1 bowl
1 chair

"Three Little Kittens have Lost Their Mittens"
3 mittens
1 pie tin

"The Little Old Lady Who Lived in a Shoe"
3 small people toys or blocks
1 shoe or boot

**Preparation**

Before the shower – none.

Before you play – according to the nursery rhyme selected, set up the target (bowl on a chair, pie tin or a shoe). Designate a throw line and have the guests form a single file line behind it.

**Introducing the Game**

To introduce the tossing game, recite or read the selected nursery rhyme from a book.

**How to Play**

Each guest will have a turn to toss 3 nursery rhyme items to land on the target. The guest with the most successes wins. In case of a tic, play additional rounds to determine a winner.

**Prizes:**  Nursery Rhyme book.

# PACIFY-HER

### Materials Needed

1 pacifier
1 large muffin pan
basket or container
paper and pen
scissors and tape

### Preparation

Before the shower – cut one circle shape for every empty space in the muffin pan. Write a different baby name on each circle and include the guest of honor's baby name. Tape the cut-outs into the muffin pan with the names facing up. Write matching names on individual pieces of paper and fold to place in the basket or container. You will have the same names in the drawing basket that appear in the muffin pan.

Before you play – make a list of the guests who will be playing the game.

### Introducing the Game

"It's a toss-up to tell which baby is crying for a pacifier."

### How to Play

Each guest will have one turn to toss the pacifier at the muffin pan. Record the name that appears in the opening the pacifier lands in next to guest's name on the list. After everyone has completed one toss of the pacifier, draw a name out of the basket to determine which baby was crying. The guest(s) who landed the pacifier in the crying baby's name win(s). If no winner is matched on the first draw, draw another name until you find a winner or winners.

**Prizes:** Bubble bath.

# PIN DROPS

### Materials Needed

1 package of diaper pins
1 empty baby food jar

### Preparation

Before the shower – none.

Before you play – set up
the empty baby food jar,
with no lid, as the target.

### Introducing the Game

"If baby is quiet, you might be able
   to hear the pins drop into the jar."

### How to Play

Each guest will have a turn to drop four diaper pins into the baby food jar.
For a fair game, everyone should stand directly over the jar, hold the diaper
pin at waist height and drop it into the baby food jar. The guest with the
most successes wins.

**Prizes:**  Fill empty baby food jars with decorative essentials, such as
buttons, safety pins of all sizes, potpourri, miniature soaps or bath beads.
Create extras in the event of tie winners or for other games.

# TEETHING RING TOSS

## Materials Needed

1 full two-liter bottle of soda
1 cooling teether

## Preparation

Before the shower – none.

Before you play – set up the two-liter soda bottle as the target. Designate a throw line and have the guests form a single file line behind it.

## Introducing the Game

"The cap's off this soda bottle if you can ring it for refreshment."

## How to Play

Each guest will have a turn to toss the teether 3 times to ring the soda bottle. The guest with the most successes wins. In case of a tie, play additional rounds to determine a winner.

**Prizes:** Bracelets.

# TOY BOX TOSS

## Materials Needed

3 to 5 soft toys
   (stuffed animals
   or squeak toys)
1 sturdy box
gift wrapping paper
scissors
tape

## Preparation

Before the shower – wrap the sides of the box with gift wrapping paper to decorate as a toy box.

Before you play – set up the toy box as a target. Designate a throw line and have the guests form a single file line behind it.

## Introducing the Game

"This clean-up chore is really a game, to see who can make it into the toy basketball hall of fame."

## How to Play

Each guest will have a turn to toss the toys into the toy box. The guest with the most successes wins. In case of a tie, play additional rounds to determine a winner.

**Prizes:** Present a toy your guests will remember from their own childhood; a yoyo, jacks, jump rope, bubbles, etc.

# BABY SONGS

## Materials Needed

1 photocopied list
   of baby song titles
   per guest
1 pencil per guest

## Preparation

Before the shower – look up song titles with the word "baby." This can be researched at the music store, in a karaoke playlist or on the Internet. Try to include classic tunes, oldies, country, rock, easy listening, disco, rap and blues for a variety of music. List the songs on a piece of paper and copy one for each guest. Be sure not to include the singer's name on the photocopied lists for the guests. Record the singer's names on a separate list for your reference only.

Before you play – hand out one baby songs list and a pencil to each guest.

## Introducing the Game

"We've named the tune of these *baby* songs, can you name the artist?"

## How to Play

Allow a time limit of 5 minutes for the guests to write down the name of the artists on the list of baby song titles. The guest with the most correct artists wins the prize. In the event of a tie, select one of the artists from the list who is very well known. Have the runners-up (all tie winners) list as many hit songs from that artist in 3 minutes on the back of their baby song game sheet. The other guests can help verify if the song titles are correct when you read the song titles aloud.

**Prizes:** CD single.

# BASEBALL OR BALLET?

## Materials Needed

1 piece of paper per guest
1 pencil per guest

## Preparation

Before the shower – study the sports page of a newspaper, review a sports magazine or search the Internet for popular athlete's names to assist you.

Before you play – choose baseball (male sports figures) or ballet (female sports figures) as the subject of the game based on baby's sonogram or arrival. Give one piece of paper and one pencil to each guest.

## Introducing the Game

"My baby's a star athlete in training, name all of the sports figures he or she can look up to."

## How to Play

Allow five minutes to list as many sports figures, male or female, on the piece of paper. Be sure to announce the famous athletes can be from any sport (past or present) and add the following suggestions: baseball, basketball, ice hockey, football, soccer, tennis, gymnastics, golf, ice skating, Olympic stars.

**Prizes:** Sport balls, miniature sport balls or free miniature golf tickets.

# DESIGNER TEDDY BEARS

## Materials Needed

1 piece of brown
   construction paper
   per guest
1 pencil per guest

## Preparation

Before the shower – none.

Before you play – give one piece
of brown construction paper and
one pencil to each guest.

## Introducing the Game

"Did you ever want to design a teddy?
Not a nightie, a teddy bear!"

## How to Play

Each guest will design a teddy by tearing the paper to make an outline of a teddy bear. To add a degree of difficulty, ask everyone to design the teddy with their hands behind their backs. The most recognizable (or best) teddy bear wins.

**Prizes:** A teddy bear.

# LUCKY GUESS

## Materials Needed

1 glass or clear plastic jar or container
1 large count package of candy, party favors or clothespins
1 piece of paper per guest
1 pencil per guest

## Preparation

Before the shower – count the items to be placed in the jar or container. Write down the winning number for your reference only.

Before you play – give one piece of paper and one pencil to each guest.

## Introducing the Game

"Take a lucky guess to see if you can count on what's inside."

## How to Play

Pass the jar or container filled with candy, party favors or clothespins around the room so everyone may get a "quick" look at what's inside. Ask the guests to write down their name and their lucky guess on the piece of paper. Collect the slips of paper and announce each lucky guess to determine who was the closest to the actual number without going over.

## Fun-Filled Suggestions:

Small jelly beans or candies in a baby's bottle.
An assortment of tiny party favors in an empty baby food jar.
Safety pins or diaper pins in a clear cosmetic bag.
Clothespins in a plastic container.

**Prizes:** The jar filled with candy, party favors or clothespins.

# NICKNAMES

## Materials Needed

1 photocopied list per guest
1 pencil per guest

## Preparation

Before the shower – as the guests RSVP by telephone, ask for their nickname as a child (or now) and make a note of it by their name. Prepare another list; on one side of the paper list each guest's name and on the other side of the paper list all of the nicknames in random order. Photocopy one "match up" game list per guest. Keep the list of the correct answers for your eyes only.

Before you play – give one photocopied game sheet and one pencil to each guest.

## Introducing the Game

"We're bringing back everyone's childhood memories with their endearing nicknames."

## How to Play

Everyone will have 8 minutes to match one guest's name to one nickname. Make an announcement to recall any clues or if anyone may have shared information to reveal their nicknames during the shower. Their personalities, hobbies and favorites may be a key to their true childhood identity.

**Prizes:** Cartoon character gifts.

# PASS THE BOOTIE

## Materials Needed

1 baby bootie
1 bag of colored candies
   (jelly beans, candy
   coated almonds, etc.)

## Preparation

Before the shower – choose pink or blue for baby as the winning color and place only one candy of that color in the bootie. Fill with various other colored candies.

Before you play – none.

## Introducing the Game

"Reach into this rainbow of colors for baby."

## How to Play

As the guests pass the bootie around the room, they are to reach into the bootie (with their eyes closed) and take out only one candy. After the bootie has been passed and everyone has one piece of candy, announce the winning color. For more than one winner, announce "pink" for a girl, "green" for eye's like Daddy's, "yellow" for baby's bassinet. Select colors to tell more about the baby and award a prize to each winner. Be sure to include only one of each winning color in the bootie

**Prizes:** Pink or blue slippers.

# SUPER SAVERS

## Materials Needed

6 coupons per guest
scissors

## Preparation

Before the shower – clip 6 or more coupons per guest of varying savings amounts.

Before you play – shuffle the coupons and pass out an even number to each guest as you would when dealing a card game.

## Introducing the Game

"Our super saver is the guest with the best savings."

## How to Play

After the coupons are passed out to each guest, ask everyone to add up the savings offered on the coupons. The guest with the highest total amount of savings is the winner. In the event of a tie, collect all of the coupons, shuffle and pass out 6 or more again to the tie guests to determine a final round winner.

**Prizes:** Award all of the coupons or a grocery store gift certificate to the super saver.

# THE WORD'S OUT

## Materials Needed

1 game sheet per guest
1 pencil per guest

## Preparation

Before the shower – select the words or phrase to use for this challenging word game; baby's full name, parent's names or a popular baby phrase. Write it on the top of the page and copy one game sheet for each guest.

Before you play – give one game sheet and one pencil to each guest. Ask everyone to write his or her name on the back of the paper.

## Introducing the Game

"How many everyday word's out of baby's name can you find?

## How to Play

Allow the guests 6 minutes to write down as many words as they can find using only the letters provided at the top of the sheet. Be sure to announce if there is only one of any letter listed, it can only be used once within the word. Ask the guests to exchange papers with one other guest and quickly grade the papers to make sure they are actual words and names that are spelled correctly. Count the total number of words and write the number at the top of the paper. The guest with the highest number is the winner.

**Prizes:** Fancy pens or pencils, pencil holder, address book or stationery.

# BABY BARGAIN SWAP

## Materials Needed

6 pairs of the exact same baby items
   (save the receipt with all of the prices listed)
pencil and paper

## Preparation

Before the shower – list the baby items and their individual prices for your reference only. List in order, beginning with the least expensive item and ending with the highest priced item.

Before you play – divide the guests into two teams. Give each team a set of the supermarket items. Ask them to sit in two rows, back to back, so each team will not see the other team's progress. Designate one team captain who will sit at the start of each row. This will be where the lowest priced item begins.

## Introducing the Game

"Everyone's a smart shopper. Work together to begin with the best baby bargains and end with the most expensive."

## How to Play

Place the baby items in a row, on the floor, in random pricing order. Each team must swap the order of the gifts until they believe the items are in a row, priced lowest to highest (lowest price item beginning in front of the team captain). If each team is incorrect after the first attempt, announce they are both wrong and baby bargain swap again. The first team to line up the items in the correct pricing order wins.

**Prizes:** Coupon organizer wallets or "shopping list" note pads.

**Gift Option:** Present all of the baby items used in the swap to mom-to-be.

# BABY BOTTLE BOWLING

## Materials Needed

10 empty baby bottles
1 ball (miniature sport ball or tennis ball)

## Preparation

Before the shower – none.

Before you play – set up the ten empty baby bottles as bowling pins; one in the front, two in the second row, three in the third row and four in the back row.

## Introducing the Game

"Line up those baby bottles for those all-night feedings to follow."

## How to Play

Each guest will have one attempt to knock down the baby bottle "pins." The player to score the highest in one roll will win the game. To break a tie game, the runners-up will roll again to determine the winner.

**Prizes:** Bowling "one free game" gift certificates.

# DIAPER STACK

## Materials Needed

2 large packages of infant size disposable diapers

## Preparation

Before the shower – none.

Before you play – divide the guests into two teams. Give each team one package of unopened diapers.

## Introducing the Game

"Let's see if your diapering skills really stack up."

## How to Play

On your mark, get set, stack! The first team to build a tall tower using all of their disposable diapers wins. If the tower tumbles, start stacking all over again. Collect the diapers used in the games and present them to the guest of honor for the new arrival.

**Prizes:** Look for baby travel size items that grown-ups can use; baby powder, baby oil or lotion, baby shampoo. These inexpensive favors can award the entire winning team.

# HOOK, LINE AND PACIFIER

## Materials Needed

1 Christmas ornament hook or small paper clip
1 one-yard length of yarn
1 pacifier with an open, ring shaped handle
1 shallow dish or pie tin

## Preparation

Before the shower – if an ornament hook is not available, bend a paper clip into the shape of a fishing hook. Tie a piece of yarn to the top of the hook to resemble a fishing line.

Before you play – place the pacifier in the dish or pan, ring side up.

## Introducing the Game

"Practice your angling skills in case baby's pacifier gets lost at sea."

## How to Play

Allow each guest only 30 seconds to hook the pacifier, reeling it in from the dish or pan. The winner is the guest with the most "catches."

**Prizes:** Decorate a small tackle box, it's a great organizer for tiny items.

# IT'S A BALLOON!

## Materials Needed

1 balloon per guest
1 piece of paper
1 marking pen
scissors

## Preparation

Before the shower – cut the piece of paper into squares, one for each guest. Determine the winning name (this will be baby's name after birth or mom-to-be's choice for baby's name before birth). Write the winning name on one piece of paper and other baby names on the remaining pieces of paper. Fold up the papers and place one of each name into a balloon. Blow up the balloons and tie. Each balloon will have a name inside.

Before you play – give each guest a blown-up balloon.

## Introducing the Game

"Everyone will be bursting with excitement on the day baby arrives."

## How to Play

Everyone will sit on their balloons to pop them and retrieve the paper inside. The guest who delivers the winning baby name will receive a prize.

**Prizes:** A chocolate or bubble gum cigar.

# JUGGLE IT

## Materials Needed

2 large laundry baskets
2 of each of the following:
  empty milk carton,
  large cereal box,
  large teddy bear,
  small tennis shoes,
  purse, toy telephone,
  newspaper, oven mitts,
  dog dish and any other
  distractions you can find
  in a pair that are lightweight
  and unbreakable.

## Preparation

Before the shower – gather the items and divide equally for two teams. Place each set in a large laundry basket.

Before you play – divide the guests into two teams and ask each team to designate a "juggler." Give each team a bag filled with daily distractions.

## Introducing the Game

"Life as a mom is a circus, or so it appears, see if you can juggle it without any tears."

## How to Play

The first team to successfully load up the "juggler" with all of the items in the laundry basket (daily distractions), without dropping any, is the winning team.

**Prizes:** Snack size animal crackers.

# TWIN DICE

## Materials Needed

2 dice
1 lightweight cereal bowl
  or pie tin
5 to 7 gifts per 12 guests

## Preparation

Before the shower – none.

Before you play – seat the guests in a circle and place the unwrapped gifts in the middle of the circle. Give the dice and bowl or tin to the first player to start the game. Designate the direction of play, counterclockwise or clockwise. Set a timer for the game to end in 5 minutes.

## Introducing the Game

"It's a roll of the dice to see if it will be twins?"

## How to Play

The starting player will roll the dice, if no doubles pass the dice and bowl to the next player. Keep rolling and passing until the first player rolls doubles, or "twins," select a gift from the center and continue to pass the dice and bowl. Each guest to roll doubles selects a gift from the center. The game will pick up speed when all of the gifts have been selected and now the guests are allowed to "steal" a gift from another player. Announce during the game the gifts must remain in view, on the player's laps, to make it easier to steal. When the timer sounds at 5 minutes, each guest will keep the gift(s) in his or her lap.

**Game Tip:** If you have more than 10 players, use two sets of game dice. Begin at opposite sides of the circle and play one set counterclockwise and the other set, clockwise.

# WATERMELON BABY

## Materials Needed

1 watermelon
1 baby blanket
1 piece of paper per guest
1 pencil per guest

## Preparation

Before the shower – when you purchase the watermelon, remember the exact weight (pounds and ounces) from the scale in the produce section of the grocery store. Wrap the watermelon in a baby blanket.

Before you play – give each guest a piece of paper and a pencil.

## Introducing the Game

"Who wants to hold the watermelon baby?"

## How to Play

The guest of honor will allow each guest to hold the "watermelon baby" for a few seconds. After everyone has had an opportunity to hold "the baby," ask each guest to write their name and the exact weight (in pounds and ounces) of the "watermelon baby." Collect the papers and award the guest with the answer closest to the actual weight (without going over) a prize.

**Prizes:** Watermelon flavored candies, lip balm or scented soap, candles.

## BABY PHOTO MATCH GAME

Ask everyone to bring a baby picture of themselves to the shower. Post all of the pictures on a posterboard and number the photos. Hand out paper and pencil to each guest. Try to match the baby photos to the guests by filling in the name of the person next to the number of the one you feel is a match. Allow the guests to walk around to see name badges or introduce themselves as they may not be acquainted with everyone at the shower. This traditional game is a great way to allow your guests the opportunity to meet and mingle.

## CAN'T SAY "BABY"

Upon arrival each guest will receive a clothespin, party favor necklace or a decorative pin. If a guest hears another guest uttering the word "baby" in any sentence, they can take their pin. Be sure to make it clear what is to be relinquished, one pin or the whole collection (if they have successfully gathered other pins prior to their slip of the word "baby"). These pins, or necklaces, are to be worn and the game played throughout the baby shower. At the end of the party, the guest with the most pins wins.

# COTTON BALL SCOOP

There are two variations for this game. The first is to have each guest take a turn scooping up cotton balls while blindfolded. Everyone will be given 30 to 60 seconds (if you have less than 10 guests, allow 60 seconds to scoop; if you have 10 or more guests, allow only 30 seconds). Supply a large plastic serving spoon and a lightweight bowl for the guest to hold in their other hand while they scoop up their successes. Scatter the cotton balls on the floor in front of the blindfolded participant. Be sure the player keeps the bowl in the air and does not use it to shovel the cotton balls into directly from the floor. The guest with the most cotton balls wins the game.

The second variation for this game is to have one volunteer scooper and allow the participant 2 minutes to fill the bowl. Before the actual start of the game, each of the remaining guests will write down their guess of how many cotton balls will be scooped into the bowl. The winner is the guest who comes closest to the actual number of cotton balls scooped into the bowl.

# DESIGNER BABY T-SHIRTS OR BIBS

Supply one white, infant size t-shirt or solid color bib to each guest. Provide non-toxic fabric markers for the guests to share to design unique apparel for baby.

## DIAPER DERBY

You will need two infant size dolls, two pairs of large athletic socks and one disposable diaper for each guest. Divide the guests into two teams. Everyone is to be seated in this relay. Supply a doll and one pair of socks to the starting player on each team. Begin the diaper derby by the first player on each team putting the socks on their hands and placing the disposable diaper on the baby. Pass the baby and the pair of socks to the next player on the team. The second player must put the socks on their hands and remove the disposable diaper and put on the new disposable diaper they were given before the start of the relay. Pass the baby and the pair of socks to the third player on the team and repeat the "quick change" for each player on the team until everyone has placed their disposable diaper on the baby. The first team to finish the diaper derby wins the game.

## DR. MOM

Give each guest a pen and a blank index card. Ask everyone to offer their best advice for the new baby by sharing words of wisdom on the front of the index card. Examples: Soothing tips for teething, how to remove laundry stains, burping techniques, remedies for colic, etc. Be sure each Dr. Mom writes their name and phone number (if available for house calls) on the back of the card. Have the guest of honor draw one of the advice cards and announce the name written on the back as the winner of a door prize.

# FEEDING TIME

Fill 6 baby bottles with equal amounts of apple juice, water or soda before the shower. Ask for volunteers to participate in this drinking contest. You will need at least two players for the competition. You may either set a timer for five minutes or you may see who finishes the bottle first. If you use a time limit, announce the time limit before the start of the game and call the game when time is up. The winner is either the guest who drank the most during feeding time or the guest who finishes the bottle first.

# GUESS THE BABY FOOD

Number 8 to 12 jars of baby food and write down the corresponding answer for each jar on a piece of paper for your reference only. Try to select different colors for a variety of main dishes, fruits and vegetables. Give each guest a piece of paper and a pencil and have them number the game sheet according to how many jars of baby food are on display. There are two traditional variations of this game, the guests can either taste the baby food or examine the closed jar and try to guess only by appearance. A wonderful alternative to the tasting of the baby food is to allow your guests to open the jar to view the consistency and smell the contents. Award the guest with the most correct answers a prize.

## IT'S IN THE BAG

Purchase 12 baby care items and place each item separately in one brown paper lunch sack. Be sure to seal the lunch sacks securely with tape. Write down the numbers one through twelve on the lunch sacks. Be sure to make a list of the corresponding items for your reference only. Give each guest a piece of paper and a pencil and have them number their game sheet accordingly. The guests will have 10 minutes to pass the items around the room and determine what is in the bag by touch only. The guest with the most correct baby care items listed wins the game.

## MEASURE MOM'S BELLY

This traditional game has become so popular that you can now purchase garland especially for this game. You may also use crepe paper (easy to tear) or toilet paper (count the squares to quickly determine a winner). These choices are better than ribbon or string as they require no scissors to be passed among the guests. Pass around the crepe or toilet paper and have everyone tear off the length they believe would fit exactly around mom-to-be's waist. After everyone has a guess in hand, measure mom-to-be's belly for the winning size. Hold up the winning length to determine which guest is the closest. For toilet paper, announce the winning number of squares.

## MEMORY TRAY

Purchase 15 to 20 small baby care items to arrange on a tray. Give each guest a piece of paper and a pencil. At game time, present the tray by placing it in the center of the room. Allow the guests to view the items for only two minutes. Remove the tray from the room and asks the guests to write down everything they can remember that was on the tray. A fun twist to this game is to present the game as described above, but have the guest of honor hold the tray instead. After the guest of honor leaves the room with the tray, have her remain in the next room. Ask questions relating to the guest of honor. Prepare your questions, and answers, in advance for a quick determination of the winner.

## MY WATER BROKE

Purchase tiny plastic babies from a party supply or craft store. Freeze them in water in ice cube trays prior to the shower. Give each guest an ice cube containing the baby party favor in a small cup of water towards the beginning of the shower. The guest whose water breaks, or ice melts, first is the winner. It will be fun to watch the guests think of ways to make the baby arrive sooner.

## MYSTERY MESSY DIAPERS

Number 8 disposable diapers 1 through 8 with a permanent marker. In a microwave, melt one kind of chocolate candy bar for each disposable diaper. Be sure to write down the number of the diaper and the corresponding candy bar on a sheet for your reference. Give each guest a piece of paper and a pencil. Make an announcement to number their game sheets from 1 to 8. Allow the guests 10 minutes to examine the contents of the sweet smelling diapers. The guest with the most correct candy bar answers wins.

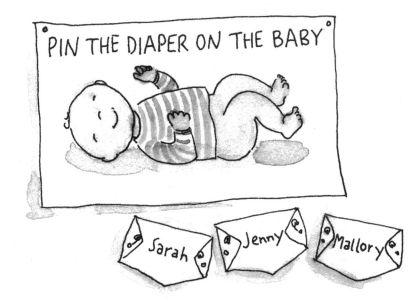

## PIN THE DIAPER ON THE BABY

This variation on the traditional Pin-the-Tail on the Donkey has been around for years. Draw a baby's outline on a piece of posterboard or use a picture of a baby from a product package or large newspaper or magazine ad. Cut out diaper shapes (see the pattern above) and write the guest's name on the diapers as if they were to be used as name tags. Each guest will have a turn to wear a blindfold and attempt to pin their diaper on the baby. You may use a piece of tape for safety's sake. The guest who tapes their diaper closest to the target area, baby's bottom, wins the prize. Retrieve the game diapers and return to each individual guest with a small safety pin to wear as a name tag.

# PRICE IS RIGHT

Purchase 6 to 10 baby care items and keep the receipt for the total amount spent on the items used for this game. Place the items on a tray and allow the guests several minutes to view the tray. Give each guest a piece of paper and a pencil to calculate their guess for the total amount of money spent on the baby care items. The guest who is closest to the correct total without going over the actual amount wins the game.

# SAFETY PIN SIFTERS

Fill a bowl with uncooked rice and small gold safety pins. Each guest will take a turn with a blindfold on to reach into the bowl and try to retrieve the safety pins. Allow 30 seconds for each player. Record each guest's name on a piece of paper and write down the number of safety pins they were able to find beside their name. The winner is the guest who retrieved the most safety pins.

# TV TRIVIA

Make a list of 10 or more television sitcom or drama families and make one copy for each guest. Include all of the children's names on one of the copies for your reference only. You can list your favorite shows, past and present. If you can't remember the names of the children, a quick search on the Internet or a look at some trivia books will help fill in your lists. Give each guest the game sheet listing only the parents of the family or title of the show. Allow the guests 5 minutes to write down as many of the children's names they can remember for each sitcom or television drama series family. The guest with the most correct children's names wins.

# BABY ANIMALS

Bring mom and baby together by writing in the number of the species next to their corresponding baby animal name. You will have five minutes to fill in the answers. The guest with the most correct animal matches wins.

(Solution on page 86)

| | | |
|---|---|---|
| 1. Alligator | _____ Kit |
| 2. Bear | _____ Cygnet |
| 3. Deer | _____ Lamb |
| 4. Eagle | _____ Fledgling |
| 5. Frog | _____ Piglet |
| 6. Goat | _____ Pup |
| 7. Goose | _____ Cub |
| 8. Gorilla | _____ Calf |
| 9. Hare | _____ Eaglet |
| 10. Horse | _____ Fawn |
| 11. Kangaroo | _____ Tadpole |
| 12. Penguin | _____ Kid |
| 13. Pig | _____ Leveret |
| 14. Pigeon | _____ Hatchling |
| 15. Platypus | _____ Infant |
| 16. Raccoon | _____ Gosling |
| 17. Seal | _____ Colt |
| 18. Sheep | _____ Squab |
| 19. Swan | _____ Puggle |
| 20. Whale | _____ Joey |

# BABY CLOTHES QUIZ

To win in style, be the first guest to figure out the fashions below and unscramble the shaded letters to announce the two-word answer to the quiz.

Snappy one-piece garment for crawlers          ▢ _ _ _ _ _ _

Knitted or crocheted baby socks          ▢ _ _ _ _ _ _

A portion of a jacket for baby boy          _ _ _ ▢ _

Style of girl pants popular in the 1950's          _ ▢ _ _ _ _ _

Keeps baby girl's hair in place          _ _ _ _ _ _ _ ▢ _

Jumpsuit for romping around          _ _ _ _ ▢ _

Baby nylons          _ _ _ ▢ _ _

A sweater for baby by another name          _ _ _ _ _ ▢ _

A Japanese robe for babies too          _ _ _ ▢ _

Cute undergarment for baby girl dress          _ ▢ _ _ _ _ _ _

Cloth accessory that protects baby apparel          _ ▢ _

All white attire for baby's dedication (two words):

_ _ _ _ _ _ _ _ _ _ ▢ _     _ _ _ _

Before disposables were invented (two words):

_ _ _ _ _     _ _ ▢ _ _ _ _

(Solution on page 86)

# BABY BINGO

Cut out these words and place them in a drawing container for the bingo caller to use at game time. Hand out a copy of the bingo grid and 15 to 20 bingo markers (mosaic marbles, coins, etc.) to each guest. After everyone has prepared their bingo playing cards, the caller will draw one word and announce the item to be marked on the card. Continue until the first guest to cover 5 squares in a row yells "Bingo!" to win the game.

| Baby Food | Blankets | Diapers | Playpen |
|---|---|---|---|
| Baby Oil | Blocks | Formula | Rattle |
| Baby Powder | Bonnet | High Chair | Rocker |
| Baby Shampoo | Booties | Jumper | Rubber Ducky |
| Baby Wipes | Bottle | Lullaby | Stork |
| Babysitter | Bumper Pad | Mobile | Stroller |
| Bassinet | Car Seat | Monitor | Swing |
| Bathtub | Crib | Nursery | Teddy Bear |
| Bib | Diaper Bag | Pacifier | Teething Ring |

| | | | | |
|---|---|---|---|---|
| | | | | |
| | | | | |
| | | FREE SPACE | | |
| | | | | |
| | | | | |

## Randomly select only one item per square

| | | | |
|---|---|---|---|
| Baby Food | Blankets | Diapers | Playpen |
| Baby Oil | Blocks | Formula | Rattle |
| Baby Powder | Bonnet | High Chair | Rocker |
| Baby Shampoo | Booties | Jumper | Rubber Ducky |
| Baby Wipes | Bottle | Lullaby | Stork |
| Babysitter | Bumper Pad | Mobile | Stroller |
| Bassinet | Car Seat | Monitor | Swing |
| Bathtub | Crib | Nursery | Teddy Bear |
| Bib | Diaper Bag | Pacifier | Teething Ring |

# PACIFIER HIDE AND SEEK

How many pacifiers can you find?
Be the first to announce the prizewinning number.
(Solution on page 87)

# PRECIOUS BABY GEMS

*Set these precious birthstones to their corresponding month.*
*The guest with the most correct "settings" will be crowned the winner.*
(Solution on page 86)

| Sapphire | Garnet | Emerald | Opal |
| Topaz | Turquoise | Aquamarine | Pearl |
| Amethyst | Diamond | Peridot | Ruby |

January _____

February _____

March _____

April _____

May _____

June _____

July _____

August _____

September _____

October _____

November _____

December _____

# SHOPPING LIST SCRAMBLE

Be the first guest to successfully unscramble
mom's shopping list and you will be the winner.

1. TOBLET _____

2. APRICFEI _____

3. BEMOIL _____

4. BSOCKL _____

5. LTREAT _____

6. HUBTTBA _____

7. DROPWE _____

8. AYBB LIO _____

9. MERBUP DAP _____

10. SPAREID _____

11. ROOTMIN _____

12. STREBA UPPM _____

13. DYDET AREB _____

14. IBESOTO _____

15. INTHEGET GRIN _____

16. LAROMFU _____

# WHAT'S IN A NAME?

Draw a line to connect these baby names to their true meaning. You will have ten minutes to determine the origin of each boy and girl name. The guest with the most correct answers wins. (Solution on page 87)

## Girls

| | |
|---|---|
| Abigail | Princess |
| Clarissa | Admired |
| Dora | Friend |
| Hannah | Gift |
| Katherine | Father's Joy |
| Miranda | Butterfly |
| Renée | Gracious |
| Ruth | Brilliant |
| Sarah | Pure |
| Vanessa | Reborn |

## Boys

| | |
|---|---|
| Brian | Gift |
| David | Peaceful |
| Derek | Protector |
| Edward | Noble |
| Jeffrey | Little King |
| Matthew | Beloved |
| Nicholas | Guardian |
| Patrick | Strength |
| Ryan | Leader |
| William | Victorious |

# BABY BLANKIES

## Materials Needed

1 or 2 receiving blankets
1 small, lightweight baby shower party favor (baby, safety pin, pacifier, etc.)
scissors
rubberbands

## How to Stage and Play

Cut 8 to 16 small squares from the receiving blanket(s) according to the number of guests in attendance. Be sure to have one square for each guest. Wrap the tiny blankets like a burrito and secure with a rubberband. In one blanket, include the party favor and mix it in with the other blankets. Everyone will select a "baby blankie" and open it up to see if they are holding the surprise party favor. Award the winner a door prize.

**Prizes:**  Everyone keeps their baby blankie to be used as a handkerchief, washcloth, (eye glass, compact disc or computer screen) dust cloth.

# BLOCK PARTY

## Materials Needed

1 baby block per guest

## How to Stage and Play

Set up the baby blocks as a centerpiece and designate one letter to be the winner. Allow each guest to select one block from the centerpiece. Announce the winning letter and award the door prize.

**Prizes:**  A fun word game from the toy aisle of a variety store.

# BRAG BOOKS

**Materials Needed**

Purses and wallets brought to the shower by the guests

**How to Stage and Play**

This door prize is awarded to the guest who has the most baby pictures in their wallet. It can be photos of their own children, grandchildren, nieces, nephews, a friend's baby. The guest with the highest number of baby photos in their purse or wallet is the winner of the door prize. If there is a tie, you can select a different category for the runners-up; youngest baby in photo, most boys or girls (to coincide with the guest of honor's baby), most studio or candid photos. Select a tiebreaker category before you see their photos.

**Prizes:** Small photo album or picture frame.

# DIAPER RAFFLE

**Materials Needed**

1 roll of raffle tickets

**How to Stage and Play**

Note on each invitation that every 25 diapers "buys" a raffle ticket for a grand door prize. You may wish to list the door prize to be awarded on the invitation to bring in more diapers. Of course, I'm sure this breaks every rule of baby shower etiquette, but guests enjoy the luck of the draw and mom-to-be will receive enough diapers to last for several months.

**Prizes:** Restaurant or day spa gift certificates and cash is always a big hit.

## DUCKLING POND

**Materials Needed**

1 baby bathtub
1 rubber duck for each guest
1 permanent, waterproof marking pen

**How to Stage and Play**

Write baby's name or the word "baby" on the bottom of one of the rubber ducks. Fill the bathtub with just enough water to allow the rubber ducks room to float. Water is optional, you may place the ducks in the bottom of the bathtub to avoid spills. Have each guest choose a duckling from the "pond." Award the door prize to the guest who selects the winning duckling.

**Prizes:** Bath beads, shower gel, scented soap.

## HAPPY BIRTHDAY!

**Materials Needed**

**How to Stage and Play**

Announce the birth date or expected due date of the guest of honor's baby. The guest with the birthday closest to baby wins the door prize.

**Prizes:** Decorative or scented candles.

# SAVE MY PLACE

**Materials Needed**

1 bookmark per guest (write name on the back of each bookmark)
1 book (baby reference book or story collection-over 100 pages)

**How to Stage and Play**

Purchase or make bookmarks (cardstock paper and stickers), one per guest. Pass the book around the room and ask the guests to "save their place" by placing the bookmark into the book. When the book is returned to the hostess, ask the guest of honor to choose a number between 1 and the number of pages in the book. Flip to the page number she selected and find the bookmark closest to the page number. Award a door prize to the winner.

**Prizes:** Any book or a journal with blank pages.

# SMELL THE ROSES

**Materials Needed**

1 rose per guest
   (be sure to remove thorns)
1 vase
1 small rubber band

**How to Stage and Play**

Select one of the roses from the bunch and wrap the rubber band around the very bottom of the stem. Place the prizewinning rose in the center of the bouquet so the rubber band is not visible. At the end of the shower, ask the guests to select a rose as a "thank you" for sharing in the festivities. Award the guest with the prizewinning rose a door prize.

**Prizes:** A vase, floral arrangement or gardening gift.

# SPECIAL DELIVERY

## Materials Needed

1 envelope per guest
1 prize per guest
  (to fit inside an envelope)
1 red marking pen

## How to Stage and Play

With the red marking pen, "postmark" the envelopes with cities and states, fun places or hospital name. Enclose in each envelope a paper party favor (bookmarks, coupons, decorative recipe cards, note cards, scrapbooking stickers and other paper prizes). Be sure to include in one of the envelopes a prizewinning note for a door prize to be awarded.

**Prizes:** Gift certificate for ice cream, coffee or a restaurant.

# SWEET SURPRISE

## Materials Needed

1 "It's a Boy" or "It's a Girl" cigar or lollipop per guest

## How to Stage and Play

Place a sticker on one of the cigars or mark the very end of one of the lollipop sticks with pink or blue marking pen as the winning treat. Hand out one to each guest at the end of the shower as a favor. Announce the winner of the door prize is the guest holding the sweet with the sticker or marking.

**Prizes:** Candy dish filled with sweet surprises.

# THANK YOU CARD "HEAD START"

## Materials Needed

1 thank you card envelope per guest
1 pen per guest

## How to Stage and Play

With the new baby's arrival, mom will be very busy. Give her a head start on sending her thank you's by asking each guest to write his or her name and address in the "send to" space on the envelope. Collect the envelopes and scatter them face down on a table for mom to choose one of the envelopes. Read the name of the addressee to announce the winner of a door prize.

**Prizes:** Note cards or stationery.

# TWO OF A KIND

## Materials Needed

1 pair of baby socks (or booties) per guest
  (make sure they vary in colors, design, size, etc.)
1 small cloth "laundry bag" (book bag)
1 large brown paper bag (decorate with shower theme)

## How to Stage and Play

Place one baby sock from each pair into the "laundry bag." Place the remaining matching socks into the large brown paper bag. Pass the "laundry bag" around the room and ask each guest to select a sock. When each guest is holding a sock, have the guest of honor select a sock from the decorated brown paper bag. The guest with the sock's mate is the winner of the door prize. Gather the socks used to play the game and present to mom as a gift for baby.

**Prizes:** Slippers or silly socks.

# READY-TO-COPY GAME SOLUTIONS

## Baby Animals

| | |
|---|---|
| 1. Alligator | 16 Kit |
| 2. Bear | 19 Cygnet |
| 3. Deer | 18 Lamb |
| 4. Eagle | 12 Fledgling |
| 5. Frog | 13 Piglet |
| 6. Goat | 17 Pup |
| 7. Goose | 2 Cub |
| 8. Gorilla | 20 Calf |
| 9. Hare | 4 Eaglet |
| 10. Horse | 3 Fawn |
| 11. Kangaroo | 5 Tadpole |
| 12. Penguin | 6 Kid |
| 13. Pig | 9 Leveret |
| 14. Pigeon | 1 Hatchling |
| 15. Platypus | 8 Infant |
| 16. Raccoon | 7 Gosling |
| 17. Seal | 10 Colt |
| 18. Sheep | 14 Squab |
| 19. Swan | 15 Puggle |
| 20. Whale | 11 Joey |

## Baby Clothes Quiz

| | |
|---|---|
| Snappy one-piece garment for crawlers | CREEPER |
| Knitted or crocheted baby socks | BOOTIES |
| A portion of a jacket for baby boy | VEST |
| Style of girl pants popular in the 1950's | CAPRIS |
| Keeps baby girl's hair in place | HEADBAND |
| Jumpsuit for romping around | ROMPER |
| Baby nylons | TIGHTS |
| A sweater for baby by another name | CARDIGAN |
| A Japanese robe for babies too | KIMONO |
| Cute undergarment for baby girl dress | BLOOMERS |
| Cloth accessory that protects baby apparel | BIB |
| All white attire for baby's dedication (two words) | |

CHRISTENING GOWN

Before disposables were invented (two words)

CLOTH DIAPERS

Two-word answer to unscrambled shaded letters:

CHANGING TABLE

## Shopping List Scramble

| | |
|---|---|
| 1. TOBLET | BOTTLE |
| 2. APRICFEI | PACIFIER |
| 3. BEMOIL | MOBILE |
| 4. BSOCKL | BLOCKS |
| 5. LTREAT | RATTLE |
| 6. HUBTTBA | BATHTUB |
| 7. DROPWE | POWDER |
| 8. AYBB LIO | BABY OIL |
| 9. MERBUP DAP | BUMPER PAD |
| 10. SPAREID | DIAPERS |
| 11. ROOTMIN | MONITOR |
| 12. STREBA UPPM | BREAST PUMP |
| 13. DYDET AREB | TEDDY BEAR |
| 14. IBESOTO | BOOTIES |
| 15. INTHEGET GRIN | TEETHING RING |
| 16. LAROMFU | FORMULA |

## *Precious Baby Gems*

| | |
|---|---|
| JANUARY | GARNET |
| FEBRUARY | AMETHYST |
| MARCH | AQUAMARINE |
| APRIL | DIAMOND |
| MAY | EMERALD |
| JUNE | PEARL |
| JULY | RUBY |
| AUGUST | PERIDOT |
| SEPTEMBER | SAPPHIRE |
| OCTOBER | OPAL |
| NOVEMBER | TOPAZ |
| DECEMBER | TURQUOISE |

# READY-TO-COPY GAME SOLUTIONS

## What's In a Name?

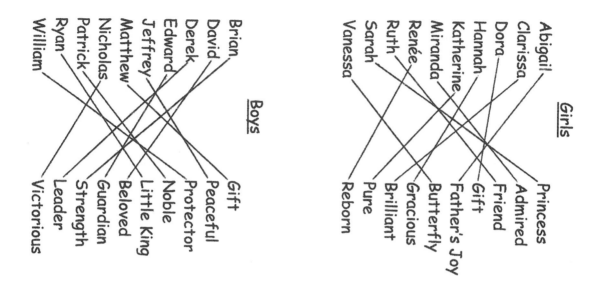

## Pacifier Hide and Seek

Answer: 36 pacifiers

# *Index*

*Also available from Funcastle Publications*

80 fun games and activities for parties, classrooms, youth groups, carnivals, company picnics, rainy days and special occasions
for ages 2 to 12